Searchlight BOOKS™

Understanding the Coronavirus

Coronavirus in Sports and Entertainment

Margaret J. Goldstein

Lerner Publications ◆ Minneapolis

Lerner Publications Company
An imprint of Lerner Publishing Group, Inc.
241 First Avenue North
Minneapolis, MN 55401 USA

For reading levels and more information, look up this title at www.lernerbooks.com.

Main body text set in Adrianna Regular.
Typeface provided by Chank.

Library of Congress Cataloging-in-Publication Data

Names: Goldstein, Margaret J., author.
Title: Coronavirus in sports and entertainment / Margaret J. Goldstein.
Description: Minneapolis : Lerner Publications , [2021] | Series: Searchlight Books -
   Understanding the Coronavirus | Includes bibliographical references and index. |
   Audience: Ages 8 -11 years | Audience: Grades 4 -6 | Summary: "The COVID-19
   pandemic changed many aspects of sports and entertainment. From closing gyms
   and stadiums to canceling concerts and postponing the Summer Olympics, readers
   will learn how the world adapted to the deadly pandemic" —Provided by publisher.
Identifiers: LCCN 2021008055 (print) | LCCN 2021008056 (ebook) |
   ISBN 9781728428505 (Library Binding) | ISBN 9781728431444 (Paperback) |
   ISBN 9781728430751 (eBook)
Subjects: LCSH: Sports—Social aspects—Juvenile literature. | Internet entertainment
   industry—Social aspects. | COVID-19 Pandemic, 2020—Juvenile literature. | Social
   change—History—21st century—Juvenile literature.
Classification: LCC GV706.5 .G635 2021 (print) | LCC GV706.5 (ebook) | DDC
   306.4/83—dc23

LC record available at https://lccn.loc.gov/2021008055
LC ebook record available at https://lccn.loc.gov/2021008056

Manufactured in the United States of America
1-49387-49491-4/26/2021

Table of Contents

Chapter 1

SHOWSTOPPER

The year 2020 began normally in the United States. Sports fans watched college and pro basketball on TV. Swimmers, gymnasts, and other athletes trained for the Summer Olympic Games. In Los Angeles, actors and production crews created TV shows and movies. Music and film lovers bought tickets for the South by Southwest arts festival in Austin, Texas. Americans went to restaurants, movie theaters, and gyms.

But life changed dramatically in March 2020. Americans learned that a new virus was spreading around the world. The virus, commonly called coronavirus, caused the disease COVID-19. Most people who got sick with COVID-19 had mild symptoms, such as aches, coughs, and fevers. But some people had trouble breathing and needed hospital care. Many patients died.

Some COVID-19 patients need ventilators to help them breathe.

The coronavirus spread from person to person. When someone with the virus coughed, sneezed, talked, or simply breathed, they released virus particles into the air. People standing nearby could get infected by breathing in the particles.

Viruses spread easily in crowded public places.

STEM Spotlight

In addition to sneezing, coughing, and talking, the coronavirus can spread from person to person through singing. In Washington State, a 122-member choir held two rehearsals in March 2020. The members sang with strength and enthusiasm. When they did, some of them released virus particles into the air, and other members inhaled them. After the rehearsals, more than fifty of the singers got sick with COVID-19. Two singers died.

Celebrities Get Sick

Both ordinary people and celebrities began to get infected. The singer P!nk announced in April 2020 that she had tested positive for COVID-19. The first professional US athlete to test positive was Utah Jazz basketball player Rudy Gobert.

P!nk was one of the first American celebrities to get COVID-19.

THE OLYMPIC GAMES WERE POSTPONED FOR THE FIRST TIME IN THEIR HISTORY DUE TO COVID-19.

▼

As more and more people got COVID-19, organizations made hard decisions. To keep spectators, athletes, and staff from infecting one another, sports leagues canceled games. To keep performers, staffers, and fans safe, entertainment venues shut down. Movie theaters, gyms, and swimming pools closed too. In late March, the International Olympic Committee postponed the 2020 Summer Olympic Games. The world of sports and entertainment screeched to a halt.

Chapter 2

ALTERNATIVES

Long before the pandemic, Americans used the internet to access entertainment. They watched TV and movies on Netflix, Amazon, and other streaming services. They listened to music on Spotify, Apple Music, and Bandcamp. When COVID-19 hit, online entertainment became even more popular. Streaming shows and music at home was much safer than going to crowded theaters or concert halls.

Musicians wanted to stay safe too. They wanted to avoid recording studios, where the virus might spread from person to person. Digital technology made it possible. Pop star Taylor Swift made two albums, *folklore* and *evermore*, from home during the pandemic. She used her own sound equipment to record vocal and instrumental tracks. Her musical partners recorded tracks from their homes as well. The artists sent the digital music files to one another. They used computers to layer the vocals and instrumentals. Sound engineers, also working from home, polished the tracks to make the final albums.

Taylor Swift won Album of the Year at the 2021 Grammy Awards for *folklore*.

Tom Hanks and Rita Wilson

Actor Tom Hanks and his wife, actress and singer Rita Wilson, were the first US celebrities diagnosed with COVID-19. After they recovered, medical researchers studied their blood plasma. The researchers found that their plasma contained antibodies that fight the coronavirus. After that, the couple regularly donated blood plasma to medical centers. Doctors injected the donated plasma into other COVID-19 patients. The antibodies in the plasma helped some patients recover more quickly.

Livestreamed music was also common during the pandemic. One event, called One World: Together at Home, featured Lady Gaga, Taylor Swift, Billie Eilish, Kacey Musgraves, Lizzo, and other stars, all performing from home. *Tonight Show* host Jimmy Fallon recorded a series of TV shows from his home during the pandemic. His young daughters goofed off for the camera. His wife was the camera operator.

Billie Eilish and FINNEAS take part in the performance *One World: Together at Home*.

THERE IS LESS RISK OF SPREADING THE VIRUS IN OUTDOOR SETTINGS.

The movie industry made adjustments because of the pandemic. Since movie theaters were shut down, film companies sent new releases right to streaming services. Some movie theaters got creative. They couldn't let audiences watch films indoors, so they projected movies onto giant outdoor screens in parking lots. People watched the movies from their cars.

Close Calls

Avoiding COVID-19 was difficult for athletes since many sports involve close contact between competitors and teammates. The National Basketball Association (NBA) was near the end of its regular season when COVID-19 hit the United States. Rather than cancel the season, the league postponed it. Then, it created a system called the NBA bubble.

The Utah Jazz and New Orleans Pelicans play in the first bubble game on July 30, 2020.

The bubble was set up at Walt Disney World in Florida. NBA players, coaches, officials, and other staff moved into hotels there. They were tested regularly for COVID-19. Anyone who tested positive had to go into quarantine. Only people who tested negative could take part in games, which took place at a sports complex in the bubble. When they weren't on the court, players and others wore face masks to keep the virus from spreading from person to person. Teams finished out the regular season and playoff games in the bubble with no fans in the stands.

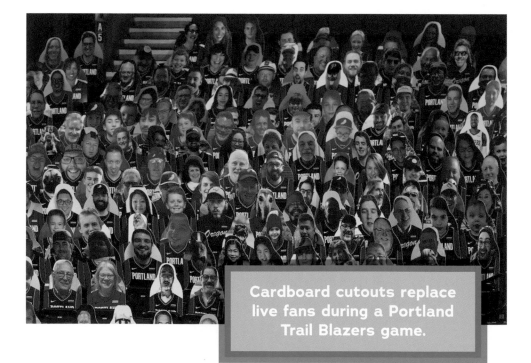

Cardboard cutouts replace live fans during a Portland Trail Blazers game.

Chapter 3

FORWARD MOTION

The pandemic continued, but entertainers and athletes wanted to get back to work. In the summer of 2020, TV and movie production started up again, but with strict rules about COVID-19. Actors wore face masks on set, except when cameras were rolling. Production crews wore masks too. Everyone practiced social distancing, standing at least 6 feet (2 m) apart to prevent infection.

Normally, film and TV producers hire many background actors, or extras, to appear in crowd scenes. But having lots of actors on set increased the risk of infection. So producers made changes. They rewrote scripts to include fewer background actors. They also used computer animation to make crowd scenes instead of hiring background actors to appear in person.

TV and movie makers use a green screen and computers so fewer actors can be used.

The Los Angeles Dodgers and the Arizona Diamondbacks play to an empty stadium.

Ballgames Come Back

After postponing its season, Major League Baseball (MLB) started up again in July 2020. But games were much different than before COVID-19. For most of the season, teams didn't allow fans in stadiums. To make the surroundings more realistic for players, the stadium staff piped in crowd noises. Some teams even placed cardboard cutouts of spectators in the stands.

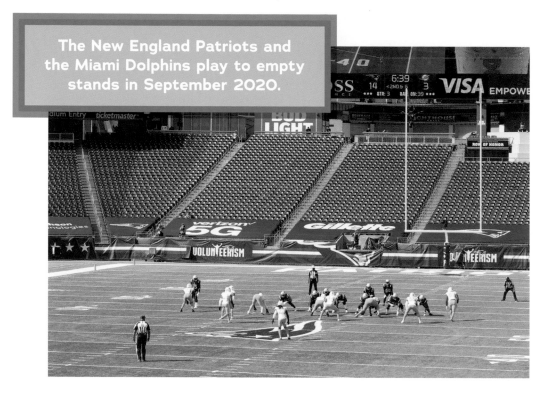

The New England Patriots and the Miami Dolphins play to empty stands in September 2020.

The National Football League (NFL) started its preseason games in August. Some teams allowed small numbers of fans in stadiums. They had to sit far from one another. Other teams could not allow any fans at games due to local or state restrictions. To keep players safe, teams enforced testing, mask wearing, and social distancing. Those who tested positive for COVID-19 had to quarantine for at least five days. New technology helped with safety. For example, on the sidelines and at practices, NFL players, coaches, and staff wore distance monitors on their wrists. The devices set off warning lights if two people got within 6 feet (2 m) of each other.

Beyoncé

During the COVID-19 pandemic, thousands of businesses shut down. Employees lost their jobs. Many people couldn't pay for housing. Singer Beyoncé (*below*) stepped in to help. She distributed money via her charity, BeyGOOD. The money paid for virus testing, helped small businesses stay afloat, and helped unemployed people make rent and mortgage payments. By the end of 2020, BeyGOOD had donated more than $6 million toward COVID-19 relief.

COVID-19 Marches On

Despite all the precautions, athletes and actors still got infected. NFL quarterback Cam Newton got the virus. So did tennis player Novak Djokovic. Entertainers who tested positive included Ellen DeGeneres, Khloé Kardashian, Robert Pattinson, and Dwayne "The Rock" Johnson.

Cam Newton had to miss a game on October 5, 2020, after testing positive for COVID-19.

Lena Dunham uses her celebrity status to warn others about COVID-19.

Most of the celebrities who got the virus had only mild symptoms. But a few stars, such as actor Lena Dunham, got extremely sick. Many stars who got sick with COVID-19 used their fame to teach others about the disease. They told their fans to wear masks and use social distancing to prevent infection.

Chapter 4

OVERTIME

In late 2020, drug companies developed vaccines to protect people from COVID-19. But vaccinating millions of Americans will take many months. Until then, sports and entertainment organizations will keep COVID-19 safety guidelines in place.

A MUSICIAN USES A HOME RECORDING STUDIO.

▼

As more and more people get vaccinated, stadiums and music venues will reopen. But the pandemic may still shape the future of sports and entertainment. For example, musicians may continue to use home recording technology to make albums. Collaborating online can be faster than traveling to and from recording studios. This approach might save money for record companies too.

STEM Spotlight

The coronavirus spreads more easily inside than outside. When people play indoor team sports, such as volleyball and basketball, the virus can spread from player to player. For this reason, many schools shut down indoor sports programs during the pandemic. Outdoor sports, especially when done by just one person, are less risky. During the pandemic, bicycling, ice-skating, snowshoeing, and other outdoor, individual sports grew more popular. People took up these sports not just to stay safe. The exercise also helped keep people physically fit and mentally calm during the COVID-19 crisis.

When the pandemic ends, life will go back to normal in many ways. Schools will restart their sports programs. Fans will go back to stadiums. The Olympics will return. Music festivals and live concerts will resume. But no one will forget the COVID-19 pandemic. Filmmakers have already started to make movies about COVID-19. Musicians have written songs to help people cope with the isolation and sadness of the pandemic. They include Luke Combs's "Six Feet Apart," Bon Jovi's "Do What You Can," and Bono's "Let Your Love Be Known."

Bon Jovi's song "Do What You Can" is about staying strong despite the hardships brought on by the COVID-19 pandemic.

The trio En Vogue performs during a livestream concert on Dec. 11, 2020.

Teamwork

During the COVID-19 pandemic, people found new and creative ways to share movies, music, art, and sports. Actors and musicians put on livestream performances on social media. Fans rooted for their favorite sports teams, even if they couldn't cheer for them in person. Athletes encouraged people to stay strong and stay safe. Despite difficulties and disruptions due to the coronavirus, sports and entertainment stars continued to inspire joy for many people.

Important Dates

March 2020   Fearing the spread of COVID-19, organizers cancel South by Southwest, a festival of music, technology, and film in Austin, Texas.

Actors Tom Hanks and Rita Wilson are the first US celebrities known to have COVID-19.

The International Olympic Committee announces that the 2020 Olympics will be postponed for one year due to COVID-19.

July 2020   After a delay of several months, the MLB starts its 2020 season but does not allow fans in stadiums.

After postponing its season in March, the NBA resumes play in the NBA bubble in Florida.

December 2020   Taylor Swift releases her ninth studio album, *evermore*, less than five months after releasing *folklore*, her eighth studio album.

Americans begin to receive COVID-19 vaccines.

Glossary

antibodies: proteins produced by the immune system to fight infection

coronavirus: a virus whose surface is covered by spiky projections

pandemic: a worldwide outbreak of a disease

positive: having an infection or illness, as indicated by a test result

quarantine: a specific time period during which people isolate themselves from others so as not to pass on a disease

social distancing: keeping a certain amount of space between yourself and others, usually 6 feet (2 m), to prevent the spread of disease from person to person

vaccine: a substance that prepares the immune system to fight off an invader, such as a virus

virus: a tiny particle that can infect living cells and cause disease

Learn More

Brundle, Joanna. *Vaccines*. New York: Enslow, 2020.

Coronavirus
https://www.brainpop.com/health/diseasesinjuriesandconditions/coronavirus/

Coronavirus Facts for Kids
https://uthsc.edu/coronavirus/documents/coronavirus-kids-fact-sheet.pdf

The Ultimate Kids' Guide to the New Coronavirus
https://www.livescience.com/coronavirus-kids-guide.html

Williams, Heather DiLorenzo. *A Lasting Impact*. Minneapolis: Lerner Publications, 2020.

Williams, Heather DiLorenzo. *Social Distancing*. Minneapolis: Lerner Publications, 2020.

Index

Photo Acknowledgments

Image credits: Tempura/Getty Images, p.5; Drazen Zigic/Getty Images, p.6; FatCamera/Getty Images, p.7; Joe Scarnici/Stringer/Getty Images, p.8; Carl Court/Staff/Getty Images, p.9; Kevin Winter/Staff/Getty Images, p.11; Amy Sussman/Staff/Getty Images, p.12; Staff/Getty Images, p.13; lechatnoir/Getty Images, p.14; Pool/Getty Images, p.15; Steph Chambers/Staff/Getty Images, p.16; Gorodenkoff/Shutterstock, p.18; Christian Petersen/Staff/Getty Images, p.19; Maddie Meyer/Staff/Getty Images, p.20; Jesse Grant/Stringer/Getty Images, p.21; Maddie Malhotra/Stringer/Getty Images, p.22; Jon Kopaloff/Stringer/Getty Images, p.23; Metech-Multimedia/Shutterstock, p.25; LightField Studios/Shutterstock, p.26; Handout/Getty Images, p.27; Frazer Harrison/Staff/Getty Images, p.28

Cover: Harry How/Staff/Getty Images